PIANO · VOCAL · GUITAR

4TH EDITION

COUNTRY
Love Songs

ISBN 0-7935-0850-9

HAL·LEONARD®
CORPORATION
7777 W. BLUEMOUND RD. P.O. BOX 13819 MILWAUKEE, WI 53213

Visit Hal Leonard Online at
www.halleonard.com

AMAZED

Words and Music by MARV GREEN,
CHRIS LINDSEY and AIMEE MAYO

Moderately slow Country Ballad

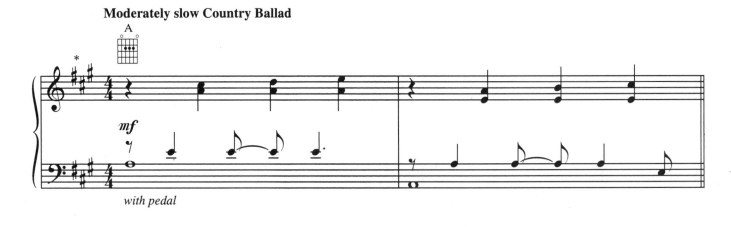

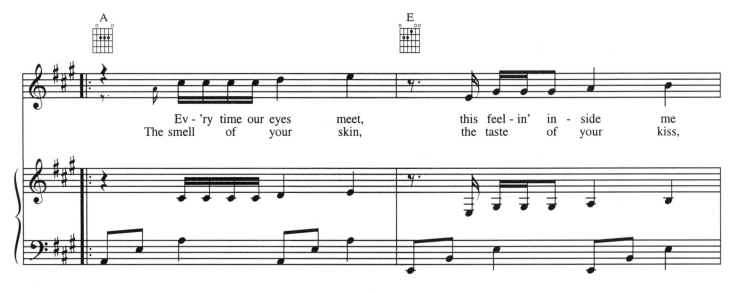

Ev - 'ry time our eyes meet, this feel - in' in - side me
The smell of your skin, the taste of your kiss,

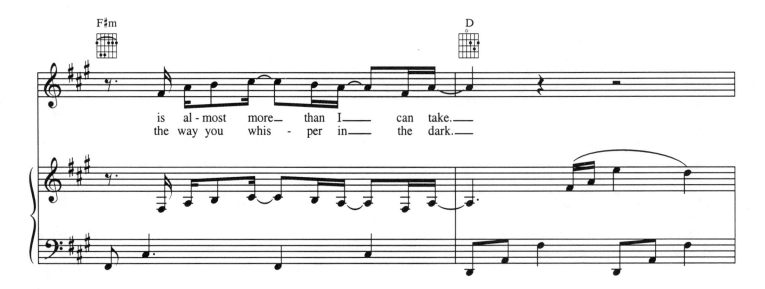

is al - most more___ than I___ can take.___
the way you whis - per in___ the dark.___

*Recorded a half step lower.

CAN'T HELP FALLING IN LOVE

Words and Music by GEORGE DAVID WEISS,
HUGO PERETTI and LUIGI CREATORE

BREATHE

Words and Music by HOLLY LAMAR
and STEPHANIE BENTLEY

Moderately fast

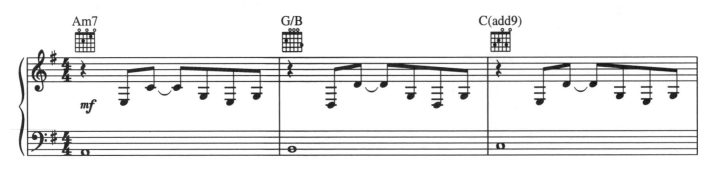

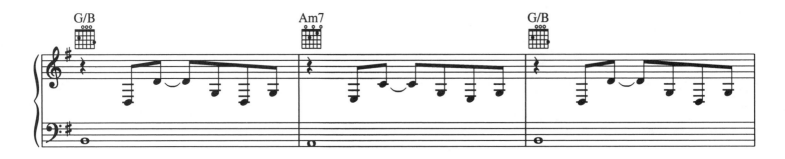

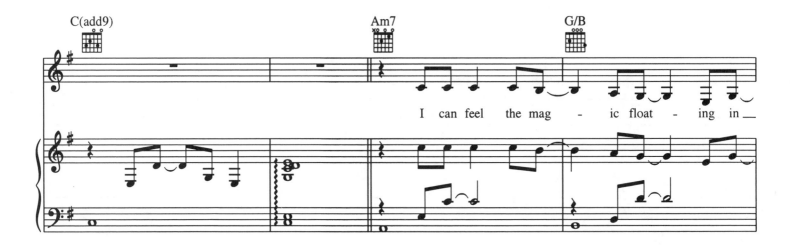

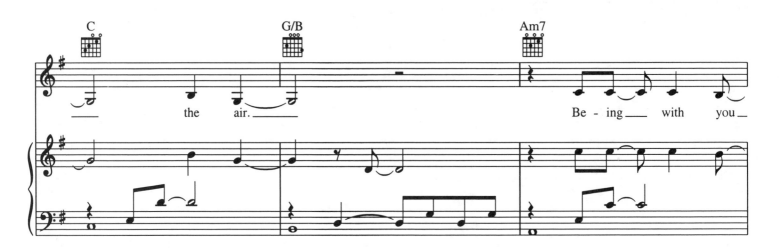

BUTTERFLY KISSES

Words and Music by RANDY THOMAS
and BOB CARLISLE

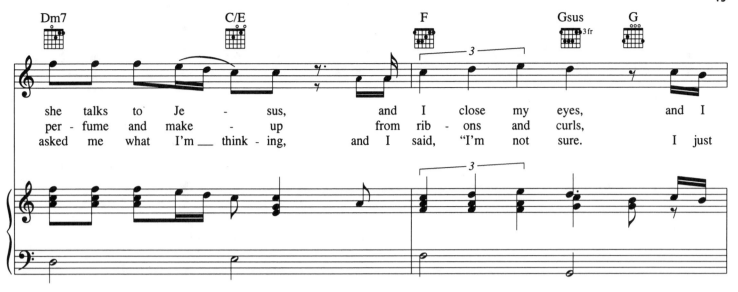

she talks to Je - sus, and I close my eyes, and I
per - fume and make - up from rib - ons and curls,
asked me what I'm __ think - ing, and I said, "I'm not sure. I just

thank God __ for all __ of the joy in my __ life.
try - ing __ her wings out in a great big world. __
feel like __ I'm los - ing my ba - by girl." __

Oh, but most of all, for but - ter - fly kiss - es __ af - ter
But I re - mem - ber but - ter - fly kiss - es __ af - ter
Then she leaned o - ver, gave me but - ter - fly kiss - es __ with her

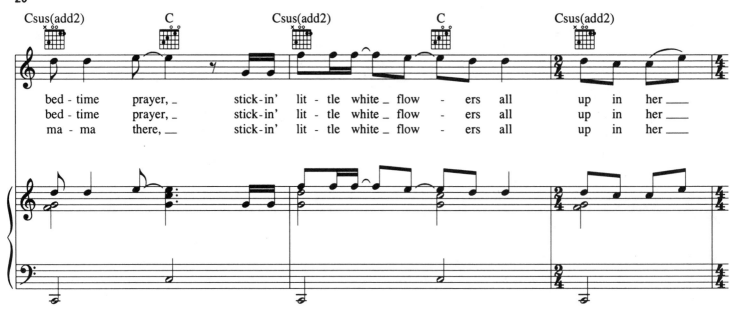

bed - time prayer, _ stick-in' lit - tle white _ flow - ers all up in her ___
bed - time prayer, _ stick-in' lit - tle white _ flow - ers all up in her ___
ma - ma there, _ stick-in' lit - tle white _ flow - ers all up in her ___

hair. "Walk be - side ___ the po - ny, dad - dy, it's
hair. "You know how much _ I love ___ you, dad - dy, but if
hair. "Walk me down _ the aisle, _ dad - dy, it's

my first ride. ___ I know the cake _ looks fun - ny, dad - dy, but
you don't mind, ___ I'm on - ly goin' _ to kiss ___ you on ___ the
just a - bout time. Does my wed - ding gown _ look pret - ty, dad - dy? Dad -

CHECK YES OR NO

Words and Music by DANNY M. WELLS
and DANA H. OGLESBY

Moderately

It start-ed way back in third __
Now we're grown up and she's __

__ grade.
__ my wife. We're

I used to sit be-side
still like two kids __ with

Em-mi-lou Hays. __
stars in our eyes. __

A pink dress,
Ain't

a match-ing bow __ in her
much changed; I still __ chase

COULD I HAVE THIS DANCE

Words and Music by WAYLAND HOLYFIELD
and BOB HOUSE

FOR THE GOOD TIMES

Words and Music by
KRIS KRISTOFFERSON

33

FOREVER AND EVER, AMEN

Words and Music by DON SCHLITZ
and PAUL OVERSTREET

I CAN LOVE YOU LIKE THAT

Words and Music by STEVE DIAMOND,
MARIBETH DERRY and JENNIFER KIMBALL

read you Cin-der-el-la, you hoped it would come true that
nev-er make a prom-ise I don't in-tend to keep. So,

one day your Prince Charm-ing would come ___ res-cue you. ___ You
when I say for-ev-er, for-ev ___ er's what I mean.

I JUST FALL IN LOVE AGAIN

Words and Music by LARRY HERBSTRITT, STEPHEN H. DORFF,
GLORIA SKLEROV and HARRY LLOYD

I NEED YOU

featured in the Epic Mini-Series JESUS

Words and Music by DENNIS MATKOSKY
and TY LACY

Vocal line written one octave higher than sung.

I NEVER KNEW LOVE

Words and Music by WILL ROBINSON
and LARRY BOONE

58

clear down to ___ my soul. _____

I nev - er knew what

beau - ty could be - hold _____ till you

IT'S YOUR LOVE

Words and Music by
STEPHONY E. SMITH

THE KEEPER OF THE STARS

Words and Music by KAREN STALEY,
DANNY MAYO and DICKEY LEE

72

LONG AS I LIVE

Words and Music by WILL ROBINSON
and RICK BOWLES

Moderately slow

mf

world's been spin-ning 'round _ since time be - gan, ___
mat - ter if there's moun - tains you can't move _

and when it stops, _ it's out of ___ my _ hands. _
or hard - er times _ than you thought you'd go _ through; _

The

LOVE CAN BUILD A BRIDGE

Words and Music by PAUL OVERSTREET,
JOHN JARVIS and NAOMI JUDD

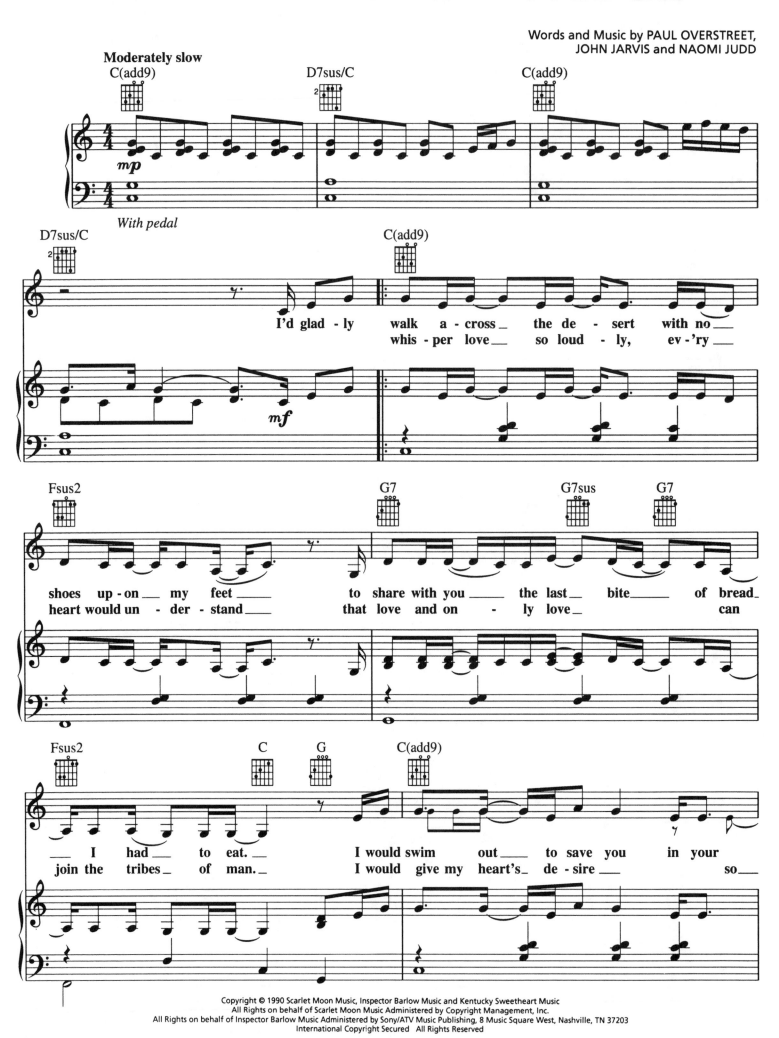

When we stand to-geth - er,____ it's our fin - est hour.____ We can do____ an - y - thing, ____ an - y - thing, ____ if we keep be - liev - in' in the pow - er.____

D.S. al Coda

CODA

Don't you think____ it's time?____

LOVE ME TENDER

Words and Music by ELVIS PRESLEY
and VERA MATSON

Moderately slow

Verse

1. Love Me Ten - der, love me sweet;
2. Love Me Ten - der, love me long;
3. Love Me Ten - der, love me dear;

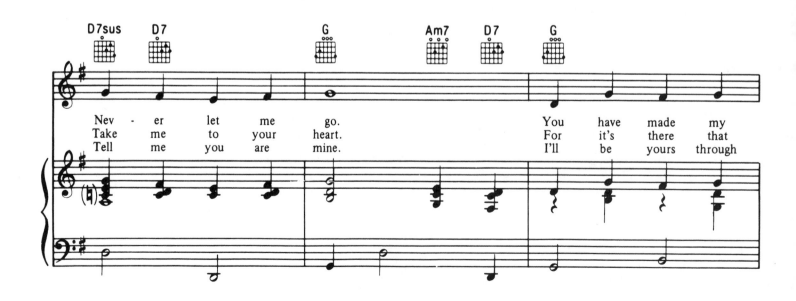

Nev - er let me go. You have made my
Take me to your heart. For it's there that
Tell me you are mine. I'll be yours through

EXTRA VERSE 4. When at last my dreams come true,
Darling, this I know:
Happiness will follow you
Everywhere you go.

LOVE OF MY LIFE

Words and Music by KEITH STEGALL
and DAN HILL

LOVE WITHOUT END, AMEN

Words and Music by
AARON G. BARKER

Moderately, with a beat

got sent home_ from school one day with a shin-er on__ my eye.
I be-came_ a fa-ther__ in the spring of eight-y - one. There

Fight-in' was__ a-gainst__ the rules__ and it did-n't mat-ter why.
was no doubt that stub-born boy__ was just like my Fa-ther's son.

When Dad got home I told that sto-ry
And when I thought__ my pa-tience had_ been_

MORE THAN YOU'LL EVER KNOW

Words and Music by
TRAVIS TRITT

I know liv-in' ___ with me ___ ain't al - ways

eas - y. I dam up e - mo-tions some men just let

flow. But, girl, when you're ___ not by ___

I'm sure you've heard _ it said ___ hearts have win-dows,

MY BEST FRIEND

Words and Music by AIMEE MAYO
and BILL LUTHER

NO DOUBT ABOUT IT

Words and Music by JOHN SCOTT SHERRILL
and STEVE SESKIN

F♯m7
A
E
No doubt a - bout it.
F♯m7
A
Oh, there ain't no doubt a - bout it.
E
F♯m7
There ain't no
A
E
Repeat ad lib. and Fade
doubt a - bout it. Oh, there ain't

ONE BOY, ONE GIRL

Words and Music by MARK ALAN SPRINGER
and SHAYE SMITH

Tenderly

He fin - 'lly gave in ___ to his friend's girl - friend ___ when she said, ___
no time at all ___ they were stand - ing there ___ in the front ___

___ "There's some - one ___ you should meet." ___
___ of a lit - tle ___ church, ___

At a
a -

crowd - ed res - t'rant way ___ cross ___ town ___ he wait - ed im - pa - tient - ly. ___
mong their friends ___ and fam - i - ly, ___ re - peat - ing those sa - cred words. ___

118

NO ONE ELSE ON EARTH

Words and Music by SAM LORBER,
STEWART HARRIS and JILL COLUCCI

THE SONG REMEMBERS WHEN

Words and Music by
HUGH PRESTWOOD

128

STAND BY ME

Words and Music by BEN E. KING,
JERRY LEIBER and MIKE STOLLER

When the

night   has come ___   and the land   is
sky   that we look up-on ___   should tum - ble and

dark   and the moon ___   is the on - ly light we
fall   and the moun - tains ___   should crum - ble   in - to the

STARS OVER TEXAS

Words and Music by PAUL NELSON,
LARRY BOONE and TRACY LAWRENCE

As you lie in _____ my arms, girl, my
know I _____ have stum-bled and

heart's on my sleeve. Words come so
caused you some tears. When you need-ed me

136

That's How You Know It's Love

Words and Music by
STEPHONY E. SMITH

THIS KISS

Words and Music by ANNIE ROBOFF,
BETH NIELSEN CHAPMAN and ROBIN LERNER

THROUGH THE YEARS

Words and Music by STEVE DORFF
and MARTY PANZER

VALENTINE

Words and Music by JACK KUGELL
and JIM BRICKMAN

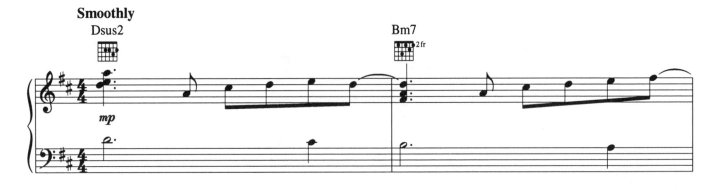

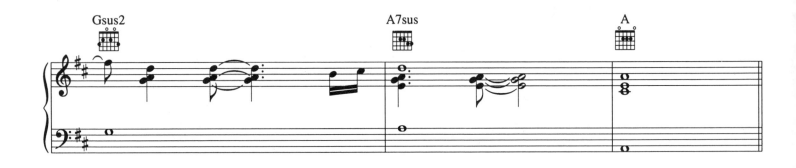

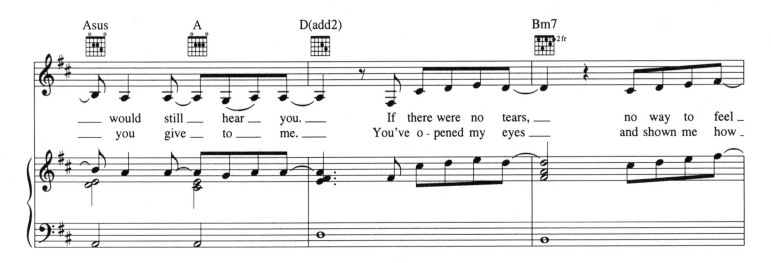

THE WAY YOU LOVE ME

Words and Music by MICHAEL DULANEY
and KEITH FOLLESE

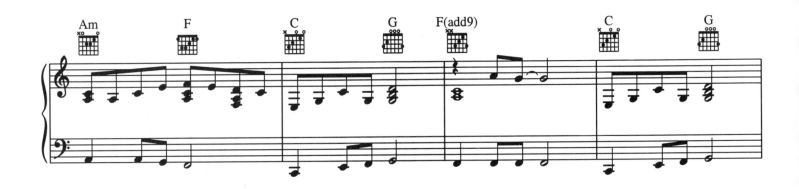

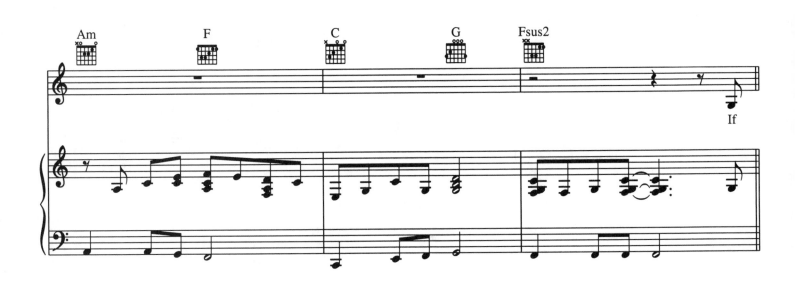

156

YOU NEEDED ME

Words and Music by
RANDY GOODRUM

160